THE LITTLE
Girl
BOOK

Paula Yates

Paula Yates (signature)

Virgin (logo)

First published in Great Britain in 1994 by
Virgin Books
an imprint of Virgin Publishing Ltd
332 Ladbroke Grove
London W10 5AH

A catalogue record for this book is available from the
British Library

ISBN 1 85227 476 X

Designed by Tony Paine
Illustrations by Diana Fisher

Typeset by Phoenix Photosetting, Chatham, Kent
Printed and bound in Great Britain by
Bath Press Ltd

We had a little baby girl,
Who made our hearts to flutter.
We used to call her Margarine:
We hadn't any but her.

Herbert R. Allport

FIRST SIGHTINGS

Name ....

....

Place of birth ....

Time and date of birth ....

....

Colour of hair ....

Colour of eyes ....

Weight at birth ....

Height at birth ....

First tooth ....

How Baby first moved along ....

....

When Baby first moved along ....

....

First words ....

....

First steps ....

MEMORIES

Favourite song ....

Favourite toy ....

Favourite story ....

....

Favourite games ....

....

First party ....

....

Favourite foods ....

....

Favourite animal ....

Favourite clothes ....

....

First friend ....

First holiday ....

Funny sayings ....

....

School Days

First day at school ....

Best friends ....

....

Favourite teacher...

First play ....

Part played and words spoken ....

....

First sports day ....

Races run ....

Favourite activity ....

....

Least liked activity ....

....

First party without accompanying adult ....

....

Funny sayings ....

....

INTRODUCTION
by Paula Yates

Fifi got up, beside herself with excitement about going out at one in the morning. Bob got us all in the car and then realised he wasn't sure where the hospital was.

One thought occurred to me when we'd finally got to the hospital and Bob told me that my doctor, the Warren Beatty of medicine, was on his way. It was that yet again I'd been taken by surprise by the whole event.

Having virtually swum the Channel the day before, then collapsed into bed, my hair had dried into a style that was a cross between something that gets hung from the altar at Harvest Festival and a Brillo pad. Not that I wish to appear vain. It was just that I kept thinking about all those photos we'd take after

the baby was born and I imagined her asking me in years to come why I'd worn a Shredded Wheat on my head when I had her.

'Call my hairdresser,' I said out of the corner of my mouth, so that the midwife couldn't hear. I was told it was three in the morning and not the best time to wheedle trend-setting teasy-weasies out of their L'Uomo Vogue lift-and-separate pyjamas. So instead, Fifi and I settled into the two single beds we'd pushed together in our room, then fell into the fitful sleep of those awaiting a big event.

The hospital day seems to start about ten minutes after the end of the previous one. No sooner had I had my breakfast, which was an ancient recipe for porridge handed down from the last days of the Bastille, than my hairdresser Nicky arrived complete with his assistant and a cloud of glamour. He plugged in his Carmen rollers next to the foetal heart monitor and started furiously tugging at my hair, which had shrunk about three inches in the night. Several nurses came into the room to have a look at what was going on. Nicky shoved Carmen rollers into everyone's hair, so they had to stay there, because it's hard to have an air of calm authority with a large pink foam curler stuck in your fringe.

Then my devilishly attractive doctor arrived and drily commented that he was delighted the labour was progressing so well. I lay back thinking he was just like one of those heroes in books called *When Hearts Cascade,* with square jaws and dark, brooding souls. Having been seen with my hair in curlers and my legs in stirrups, it is hardly likely I'll be shown this tempestuous side of him, though.

After he'd left, I realised that something in my drip was definitely disagreeing with the large quantity of grapes and chocolate which Fifi and I had consumed after breakfast, so I had to ask everyone else to leave while I threw up. I wished I was truly glamorous like Zsa Zsa Gabor, who I'm sure never throws up while she's having her hair done.

Fifi was present while her new sister was born. She was a very active participant, standing on a chair next to the bed, shouting 'Push, push, push,' like a very small cox in the Oxford and Cambridge Boat Race. She mainly

wanted me to hurry so that she could eat the mint which had fallen down the side of the bed. I felt like I was definitely crossing the pain barrier.

'I feel like Ben Johnson,' I panted. 'Well, you're drugged up enough,' said Bob. 'Oh, every one a Maserati,' I snapped back like knicker elastic. 'Who's bought a Maserati?' asked my doctor, looking up from halfway under the bed . . . This illustrates the pointlessness of trying to hold conversations during labour.

Peaches was born, looking perfect and gorgeous, just like a little peach. The doctor said it was a girl. Fifi fell off her chair, cheering, and came over to my bed. 'Can I have my mint now?' she asked.

FIRST
SIGHTINGS

We were never clear in advance how we would cope with parenthood but we were very excited. Paula carried on working until the last moment. It was odd to see her head working away at one thing while her body got on with something entirely separate. On one thing we were quite adamant. We did not want to get involved with any of the post-hippy Hampstead style of parenting with fathers being trained in the art of acting as 'coach' for the big event. I had no desire to lie on the floor, like a prat, learning how to breathe. I was going to have *a* baby, I wasn't going to have *the* baby and there was no point in pretending I was. Paula wanted me pacing up and down outside in the corridor, or running off for kebabs or pieces of coal or whatever pregnant women desired. I concurred and told her I subscribed to the Evelyn Waugh school of fatherhood – the chap buggers off to Abyssinia and then sends a telegram saying 'Have you had your child yet and what have you called it?' . . .

Then Fifi came out and they plonked her, covered in blood, on Paula's tummy. 'Oh look,' she said. 'Isn't it sweet?'

16

The baby was quiet so the doctor flicked her toe to make sure she wasn't dumb. She gave a little squawk. Paula was cuddling her and examining every square inch of her hands and face.

Then it occurred to me to ask, 'What is it?'

'Oh yes,' said the doctor, having a look, 'it's a little girl.'

I stood and tried to imagine what she would be like as an old lady. I wasn't overwhelmed by the 'miracle of birth', just fascinated. It had seemed to me to be very animalistic, but not at all undignified. Corny as it sounds, I immediately felt very protective towards them both.

I watched as Paula gorged herself on a box of Turkish Delight and drank two bottles of fizzy apple juice which had been transferred into old champagne bottles for the occasion. Then she was sick.

Is That It? by Bob Geldof

I was born in the middle of a snowstorm on Saturday, 30 January 1937. My mother was in a maternity clinic in Blackheath, London, at the time, about six o'clock in the evening, and my father was fighting a duel with Laurence Olivier at the Old Vic. Laertes versus Hamlet. Someone signalled to my father from the wings 'It's a girl,' and at the curtain call Olivier stepped forward and announced to the audience that Laertes had a daughter. My father was quietly rather proud of this story. He told it to my mother, and according to her Olivier said, 'Ladies and gentlemen, tonight a great actress has been born, Laertes has a daughter.'

An Autobiography by Vanessa Redgrave

THE BIRTH OF ELIZABETH TAYLOR

After thanking God for a girl, the mother fell into a deep sleep of exhaustion and contentment. But on awakening, she discovered things had not gone as smoothly this time. The child looked, well, 'funny' – in the sense of peculiar, not droll. Quite alarming, in fact. Her eyes were screwed tight shut, though that was commonplace among the newborn. But across her shoulders and upper arms was a thin down of black hair. Hypertrichosis, said the doctor reassuringly, a chromosomal variant: it would soon disappear. In fact, it was to recur at intervals for years. Mrs Taylor blamed herself for this deficiency in the baby; she had not been imbibing beautiful thoughts of the requisite strength.

Elizabeth by Alexander Walker

19

TO MY DAUGHTER

Bright clasp of her whole hand around my finger,
My daughter, as we walk together now.
All my life I'll feel a ring invisibly
Circle this bone with shining: when she is grown
Far from today as her eyes are far already.

Stephen Spender

MY BABY

My baby has a mottled fist,
My baby has a neck in creases;
My baby kisses and is kissed,
For he's the very thing for kisses.

Christina Rossetti

I was continually amazed by the way in which I could watch for hours nothing but the small movements of her hands, and the fleeting expressions of her face. She was a very happy child, and once she learned to smile, she never stopped; at first she would smile at anything, at parking meters and dogs and strangers, but as she grew older she began to favour me, and nothing gave me more delight than her evident preference. I suppose I had not really expected her to dislike and resent me from birth, though I was quite prepared for resentment to follow later on, but I certainly had not anticipated such wreathing, dazzling gaiety of affection from her whenever I happened to catch her eye. Gradually I began to realise that she liked me, that she had no option to liking me, and that unless I took great pains to alienate her she would go on liking me, for a couple of years at least. It was very pleasant to receive such uncritical love, because it left me free to bestow love; my kisses were met by small warm rubbery unrejecting cheeks and soft dovey mumblings of delight.

The Millstone by Margaret Drabble

The first visit to a house made by a baby, it is given an egg, salt and sixpence. The egg is the sign of the Trinity, being made up of three, shell, white and yolk, also the egg comes to life again and therefore is the promise of immortality. Salt signifies salubrity of mind and body. Silver means money and the needful things of life.

Dictionary of Superstitions,
ed. Iona Opie and Moira Tatem

When children first leave their mother's room, they must go upstairs before they go downstairs, otherwise they will never rise in the world. Of course it frequently happens that . . . the mother's room is the highest in the house. In this case the difficulty is met by the nurse setting a chair, and stepping upon that with the child in her arms as she leaves the room.

Dictionary of Superstitions,
ed. Iona Opie and Moira Tatem

If the mother was

Rosy and merry	Pale and pensive
Heavier on the right side and carrying high	Heavier on the left side and carrying low
Of cool and humid temperament	Of dry and hot temperament

If the mother had

Pains on the right side of the womb	Pains on the left side of the womb
The right breast harder and firmer	The left breast larger
Red, hard, raised nipples	Paler, more drooping nipples
Thick white milk oozing from the breast	Pale, dilute milk

then

It would be a boy   It would be a girl

History of Childbirth by Jacques Gelis

'My mother was kind of afraid to have a third child,' Shirley Temple was later to recall, 'because she wanted a girl but was afraid she would have another boy. So my dad went to the family doctor, and he said, "If you have your tonsils out, you will have a girl." So they removed my dad's tonsils, and they grew back. He had to have them out a second time, and nine months after the second operation I was born. There is no medical reason for the story, but I think it's funny.'

Shirley Temple: American Princess by Anne Edwards

The Honourable Diana Spencer was born late on the afternoon of 1 July 1961, the third daughter of Viscount Althorp, then aged 37, and Viscountess Althorp, twelve years his junior. She weighed 7lb 12oz and while her father expressed his delight at a 'perfect physical specimen' there was no hiding the sense of anticlimax, if not downright disappointment, in the family that the new arrival was not the longed-for male heir who would carry on the Spencer name. Such was the anticipation of a boy that the couple hadn't considered any girls' names. A week later they settled on 'Diana Frances', after the infant's mother and a Spencer ancestress.

Diana: Her True Story by Andrew Morton

WHAT GOOD ARE GIRLS TO ME?

I wanted someone who would play at trains,
And splash about in puddles when it rains.
And make mud-pies when Ellen isn't looking.
(Or creep into the kitchen when she's cooking,)
And hide in corners on the stairs at night
And then jump out, and give Aunt Jane a fright.

I only wanted just a boy like me,
And Mummie, when I told her, said she'd see.
I rather counted on her, wouldn't you?
And went and planned a lot of things to do . . .
And now they're upside down and in a whirl
'Cos Mummie's gone and bought a baby girl!

Jennie Dunbar

A baby that frequently smacked its lips was believed to have been born with some unsatisfied craving which the mother had experienced during pregnancy. The remedy was a little sacramental wine. And for thrush, a live frog sewn in a muslin bag and given to the child to suck was considered a certain cure, the frog drawing off the thrush and dying in the process. That sucking a live frog might make the child choke was not even contemplated, nor was it considered possible that some of these country-bred notions might contribute to the high rate of deaths in early childhood.

Children of the Great Country Houses
by Adeline Hartcup

A BABY'S HANDS

A baby's hands, like rosebuds furled
Whence yet no leaf expands,
Ope if you touch, though close upcurled,
A baby's hands.

Then, as fast as a warrior's grip their brands
When battle bolt is hurled,
They close, clenched hard like tightening bands.

No rosebuds yet dawn impearled
Match, even in loveliest lands,
The sweetest flowers in all the world –
A baby's hands.

Algernon Charles Swinburne

NESTLING TIME

Nestling closely, while kisses sweet
Fall on the dainty hands and feet
As Mother is making all ready for bed
And slumber, her wee little 'sleepy head'.

Oh, nestling hour, so sweet, so blest,
When comes my birdling to her nest!
How we love it, my baby and I,
As we sing in the starshine our 'lullaby'.

Mary D. Brice

The midwife asked me if I would like to see the child. 'Please,' I said gratefully, and she went away and came back with my daughter wrapped up in a small grey bloodstained blanket, and with a ticket saying Stacey round her ankle. She put her in my arms and I sat there looking at her, and her great wide blue eyes looked at me with seeming recognition, and what I felt it is pointless to try to describe. Love, I suppose one might call it, and the first of my life.

The Millstone by Margaret Drabble

Monday's child is fair of face,
Tuesday's child is full of grace,
Wednesday's child is full of woe,
Thursday's child has far to go,
Friday's child is loving and giving,
Saturday's child works hard for a living,
But the child that is born on the Sabbath day
Is bonny and blithe, and good and gay.

28

Nine months later, our daughter, Francesca Hilton, was born and when I held her in my arms it was one of the happiest days I've ever known. I'd never dreamed about motherhood or babies, but when I looked into Francesca's little face I felt complete.

Since then, I've loved Francesca every day of her life, even if our relationship has sometimes been stormy. She is strong-willed and talented, intelligent, a gifted comedienne, and a good horsewoman.

One Lifetime Is Not Enough by Zsa Zsa Gabor

ENID BLYTON AS A BABY

Thomas delighted in his young daughter, so like both in appearance and temperament. She had the same dark hair, alert brown eyes and sensitive, highly-strung nature, intent upon seeking out all life had to offer. Almost from the beginning he felt a special bond had been welded between them, and he was often to tell

29

her of the occasion on which he was convinced he had saved her life. She was barely three months old at the time and dangerously ill with whooping cough. The doctor, when called on that cold November evening, had looked grave. Shaking his head sadly, he had told Thomas and Theresa that he doubted if their baby girl would survive until the morning, but Thomas refused to accept the doctor's opinion. He took the sick infant from his wife's arms and all through that cold winter night sat cradling her to him, keeping out the cold and willing her to stay alive. In the early hours when the crisis had passed and he had finally been persuaded to go to bed he had lain awake for some time, exhilarated by the thought that he had undoubtedly saved his daughter's life. Enid loved hearing this story and would ask him to repeat it to her many times.

Enid Blyton by Barbara Stoney

NURSE'S SONG

When the voices of children are heard on the
    green
And laughing is heard on the hill,
My heart is at rest within my breast
And everything else is still.

'Then come home, my children, the sun is gone
    down
And the dews of night arise;
Come, come, leave off play, and let us away
Till the morning appears in the skies.'

'No, no, let us play, for it is yet day
And we cannot go to sleep;
Besides, in the sky the little birds fly
And the hills are all cover'd with sheep.'

'Well, well, go & play till the light fades away
And then go home to bed.'
The little ones leaped & shouted & laugh'd
And all the hills echoed.

William Blake

ENID BLYTON'S ANNOUNCEMENT OF HER NEW BABY

A lovely new pet has come to Old Thatch. Some of you have heard the news already, but I know a great many of you have not, because the pet arrived in the holidays. You can have three guesses – what is it? I am sure you are nearly all wrong, so I must tell you. Well, the new pet is a little baby girl! As many of you know, I am not really *Miss* Blyton, because I am married, and I am so pleased that a baby has come to live with me, because you all know how much I love boys and girls – and it is lovely to have one that really belongs to *me* and not to some other mother and father . . .

This then was my daughter, born in the autumn and a late fall into my life, lying purple and dented like a little bruised plum, as though she'd been lightly trodden in the grass and forgotten.

The Matron picked her up and she came suddenly alive, her bent legs kicking crabwise, and the first living gesture I saw was a thin wringing of hands accompanied by a far-out Hebridean lament.

This moment of meeting seemed to be a birthtime for both of us; her first and my second life. Nothing, I knew, could ever be the same again, and I think I was reasonably shaken. I peered intently at her, looking for familiar signs, but she was as convulsed as an Aztec idol. Was this really my daughter, this purple concentration of grief, this blind and protesting dwarf?

Then they handed her to me, stiff and howling, and I held her for the first time and kissed her, and she went still and quiet as though by instinctive guile, and I was instantly enslaved by the flattery of my powers . . .

She was of course just an ordinary miracle, but was also the particular late wonder of my life. So almost every night, at first, I'd take her to bed like a book and lie close and study her. Her dark blue eyes would stare straight into mine, but off-centre, not seeing me . . .

Here she was then, my daughter, here alive, the one I must possess and guard. A year before this space had been empty, not even a hope of her was in it. Now she was here, brand new, with our name upon her, and no one could call in the night to reclaim her.

She was here for good, her life stretching before us, and so new I couldn't leave her alone.

Two Women by Laurie Lee

Love me – I love you,
　　Love me, my baby;
Sing it high, sing it low,
　　Sing it as may be.

Mother's arms under you;
　　Her eyes above you;
Sing it high, sing it low,
　　Love me – I love you.

Christina Rossetti

34

CHOOSING A NAME

I have got a new-born sister;
I was nigh the first that kissed her.
When the nursing woman brought her
To papa, his infant daughter,
How papa's dear eye did glisten!
She will shortly be to christen:
And papa has made the offer,
I shall have the naming of her.

Now I wonder what would please her,
Charlotte, Julia, or Louisa.
Ann and Mary, they're too common;
Joan's too formal for a woman;
Jane's a prettier name beside;
But we had a Jane that died.
They would say, if 'twas Rebecca,
That she was a little Quaker.
Edith's pretty, but that looks
Better in old English books;
Ellen's left off long ago;
Blanche is out of fashion now.
None that I have named as yet
Are so good as Margaret.

Emily is neat and fine.
What do you think of Caroline?
How I'm puzzled and perplexed
What to choose or think of next!
I am in a little fever.
Lest the name that I shall give her
Should disgrace her or defame her,
I will leave papa to name her.

Charles and Mary Lamb

Some time later my mother decided she was beginning the 'change' and went to the doctor. He examined her and beamed 'Congratulations!' Mother looked puzzled. She was five months pregnant. Typically she held on to me past 1 April – 'No child of mine is being born on April Fools' Day!' – but on the evening of 3 April, she announced to my father that she was going to get on and have this child. She drank castor oil and scrubbed the kitchen floor and I was born three and a half hours later.

Talking to Myself by Anna Raeburn

Mrs Bird thought, as the music floated in upon her gentle sleep, that she had slipped into heaven with her new baby, and that the angels were bidding them welcome. But the tiny bundle by her side stirred a little, and though it was scarcely more than the ruffling of a feather, she awoke; for the mother-ear is so close to the heart that it can hear the faintest whisper of a child.

She opened her eyes and drew the baby closer. It looked like a rose dipped in milk, she thought, this pink and white blossom of girlhood, or like a pink cherub, with its halo of pale yellow hair, finer than floss silk. '*Carol, brothers, carol,/Carol joyfully,/Carol the good tidings,/Carol merrily!*'

The voices were brimming over with joy.

'Why, my baby,' whispered Mrs Bird in soft surprise, 'I had forgotten what day it was. You are a little Christmas child, and we will name you "Carol" – mother's little Christmas Carol!'

The Birds' Christmas Carol
by Kate Douglas Wiggin

THE BIRTHNIGHT

Dearest, it was a night
That in its darkness rocked Orion's stars;
A sighing wind ran faintly white
Along the willows, and the cedar boughs
Laid their wide hands in stealthy peace across
The starry silence of their antique moss:
No sound save rushing air
Cold, yet all sweet with Spring,
And in thy mother's arms, crouched weeping
   there,
       Thou, lovely thing.

                        Walter de la Mare

I was surprised to think that such a very new child could make so much noise, and I ran straight indoors and straight upstairs and straight into my mother's bedroom. And there was my good kind mother sitting up in bed smiling and smiling, and there, in a cot that used to be my old cot, was my new cross little sister crying and crying!

My mother said, 'Sh-sh, baby, here is your big sister come to see you.' My mother lifted my naughty little baby sister out of the cot, and my little sister stopped crying at once.

My mother said, 'Come and look.'

My little sister was wrapped up in a big woolly white shawl, and my mother undid the shawl and there was my little sister! When my mother put her down on the bed, my little sister began to CRY AGAIN.

She was a little, little red baby, crying and crying.

'Waah-waah, waah-waah,' – like that. Isn't it a nasty noise?

My little sister had tiny hands and tiny little feet. She went on crying and crying, and curling up her toes, and beating with her arms in a very cross way.

My mother said, 'She likes being lifted up and cuddled. She is a very good baby when she is being cuddled and fussed, but when I put her down she cries and cries. She is an *artful pussy*,' my mother said.

My Naughty Little Sister
by Dorothy Edwards

39

We called the child Fifi Trixibelle, for me after Auntie Fifi, who had never discouraged me from doing anything, and for Paula because she had always fancied the idea of being a Southern belle. With a name like that, we thought, she could do anything: 'And this year's Nobel Prize for Physics has been awarded to Dr Fifi Trixibelle Geldof.' Other people felt sorry for the child being inflicted with that name, but they didn't grow up as Robert Frederick Zenon Geldof. Most people when they heard my third name wondered why my father had named me after an inert gas.

Is That It? by Bob Geldof

BORN YESTERDAY: FOR SALLY AMIS

Tightly-folded bud,
I have wished you something
None of the others would:
Not the usual stuff
About being beautiful,

40

Or running off a spring
Of innocence and love –
They will all wish you that,
And should it prove possible,
Well, you're a lucky girl.

But if it shouldn't, then
May you be ordinary;
Have, like other women,
An average of talents:
Not ugly, not good-looking,
Nothing uncustomary
To pull you off your balance,
That, unworkable itself,
Stops all the rest from working.
In fact, may you be dull –
If that is what a skilled,
Vigilant, flexible,
Unemphasised, enthralled
Catching of happiness is called.

Philip Larkin

41

INFANT JOY

'I have no name:
I am but two days old.'
What shall I call thee?
'I happy am,
Joy is my name.'
Sweet joy befall thee!

Pretty joy!
Sweet joy but two days old,
Sweet joy I call thee:
Thou dost smile,
I sing the while,
Sweet joy befall thee!

William Blake

REMEMBRANCES
OF CHILDHOOD

In her early adolescence, Madonna cut off her shoulder-length brown hair, pierced her ears, and wore oddly coloured knee socks. She finally burst out of the fashion closet at a school talent show when she shocked her father by dancing in a bikini with fluorescent flowers painted all over her body.

Attending ballet classes in Rochester when she was fourteen, Madonna met a teacher who was to become the first great direct influence on her life: the late Christopher Flynn. He recognised that there was something special about Madonna, even though 'she was very young . . . barely out of adolescence, a plain little child with short, kind of dishwater blonde hair. She looked like the most innocent child in the world.'

Madonna: The Style Book by Debbi Voller

NOSES

I looked in the mirror
and looked at my nose:
it's the funniest thing,
the way it grows
stuck right out where all of it shows
with two little holes where the breathing goes.

I looked in the mirror
and saw in there
the end of my chin
and the start of my hair
and between there isn't much space to spare
with my nose, like a handle, sticking there.

If ever you want
to giggle and shout
and can't think of what
to do it about,
just look in the mirror and then, no doubt,
you'll see how funny YOUR nose sticks out!

Aileen Fisher

Mirror, mirror, tell me,
    Am I pretty or plain?
Or am I downright ugly
    And ugly to remain?
Shall I marry a gentleman?
    Shall I marry a clown?
Or shall I marry old Knives and Scissors
    Shouting through the town?

In the winter we would sit inside with our oddment boxes, small collections of tiny things kept in toffee tins. These were stamps, marbles, china ornaments, little dolls, hair clips and the ubiquitous manicure sets. Once a week we would be called for hair washing – Miss Stanford, long fingers red from the water, plunged our heads into boiling basins and scrubbed our scalps with Coal Tar Soap to keep nits at bay. Then we roasted in front of an electric bar fire till the hair was dry and our faces scarlet.

Stare Back and Smile by Joanna Lumley

IN THE MIRROR

In the mirror
On the wall,
There's a face
I always see;
Round and pink,
And rather small,
Looking back again
At me.

It is very
Rude to stare,
But she never
Thinks of that,
For her eyes are
Always there;
What can she be
Looking at?

Elizabeth Fleming

I was timid and self-effacing. To make matters worse I was ugly. My hair was thin. I wore spectacles. I had to have a brace on my teeth. And I even got eczema whenever I was especially worried. I was always paralysed with fear when my parents invited their friends' children round for parties or took me out on their social calls. In Paris, in that class, many parents were strict, but mine were stricter than most. They wanted me to become a very well-educated, cultured and, I think, rather boring girl. My education was both severe and indulgent. It left me quite unprepared for life as I found it. I hated lessons, but I worked hard because my parents wished me to do well.

Brigitte Bardot

Halfway down the stairs
Is a stair
Where I sit.
There isn't any
Other stair
Quite like
It.
I'm not at the bottom,
I'm not at the top;
So this is the stair
Where
I always
Stop.

Halfway up the stairs
Isn't up,
And isn't down.
It isn't in the nursery,
It isn't in the town.
And all sorts of funny thoughts
Run round my head:
'It isn't really
Anywhere!
It's somewhere else
Instead!'

A. A. Milne

'Curiouser and curiouser!' cried Alice (she was so much surprised, that for a moment she quite forgot how to speak good English); 'now I'm opening out like the largest telescope that ever was! Good-bye, feet!' (for when she looked down at her feet, they seemed to be almost out of sight, they were getting so far off). 'Oh, my poor little feet, I wonder who will put on your shoes and stockings for you now, dears? I'm sure *I* shan't be able! I shall be a great deal too far off to trouble myself about you: you must manage the best way you can – but I must be kind to them,' thought Alice, 'or perhaps they won't walk the way I want to go! Let me see: I'll give them a new pair of boots every Christmas.'

Alice's Adventures in Wonderland by Lewis Carroll

When the V-1 rockets started we had to queue up at Fulham town hall for our gas masks. For Lynn there was a gas cradle. She was laid inside and the lid closed down over her so that she resembled a miniature Snow White through the glass window. Corin had a gas mask like Mickey Mouse. Nanny growled and prowled like a bear in her mask. Thinking it was very funny we never asked what the masks were for. The doodlebugs and the later V-2s thumped down day and night. We saw strange men with yellow diamonds sewn on the backs of their brown overalls clearing away the rubble in the streets. Nanny said they were 'internees'.

An Autobiography by Vanessa Redgrave

Ring-a-ring o' roses,
A pocket full of posies,
A-tishoo! A-tishoo!
We all fall down.

GRETA GARBO

'I cannot put a year to the time that my love for the theatre first began. It seems as if I have always carried it inside me. Already when I was very small and could still hardly talk I had a certain mania to paint – not on paper, as most children do, but on my own face. With the aid of a small paintbox my father had given me I painted my lips and face, believing that this is what real actresses do. No one in my family could escape my paintbrush. Then I forced them, together with me, to perform big dramas, amid screams which would make any spectator doubt that I was in possession of my senses.

'I never enjoyed playing with others, even with my sister and brother, but preferred to sit alone with my dolls and picture books, and I found my greatest pleasure in my childish dreams. Unfortunately I am still the same now – finding it difficult to adjust to other people.'

The Divine Garbo
by Frederick Sands and Sven Broman

Mary, Mary, quite contrary,
How does your garden grow?
With silver bells and cockle shells,
And pretty maids all in a row.

Although a quiet, reflective child, given to day-dreaming and dressing up in her mother's clothes, [Audrey] was not the 'sweet little girl' type. She was thin, and frequently sickly, but tomboyish in spirit and would race her brothers to scale the trees and jump the fences on the estate. And, unlike most other little girls, she bore no regard for dolls. When, from time to time, the Baroness tried to interest her daughter in such playthings, she would leave them in a pile in the nursery, complaining 'They're so *silly*', and years later she would confess, 'They just never seemed real to me.' For the remainder of her life she would be a realist.

Audrey Hepburn by Ian Woodward

Like her elder sisters, Diana was on horseback at three and soon developed a passion for animals, the smaller the better. She had pet hamsters, rabbits, guinea pigs, her cat Marmalade . . . and, as her mother recalls, 'anything in a small cage'. When one of her menagerie died, Diana dutifully performed a burial ceremony. While goldfish were flushed down the lavatory, she normally placed her other dead pets in a cardboard shoe box, dug a hole beneath the spreading cedar tree on the lawn and laid them to rest. Finally, she placed a makeshift cross above their grave.

Diana: Her True Story by Andrew Morton

The silence was finally broken by Violet Elizabeth who raised her voice again shrill and unabashed.

'I don't thee what good a newthpaper ith without any crimeth.'

They looked at her. She met their gaze unflinchingly and repeated her statement.

'I don't thee what good a newthpaper ith without any crimeth.'

'I wish you'd stop int'ruptin' an' int'ruptin' an' *int'ruptin'*,' said William. 'How d'you think we're goin' to get any work done with you int'ruptin' an' *int'ruptin'*.' But he added, because her words had really intrigued him, 'What d'you mean sayin' that a newspaper isn't any good without crimes?'

'Thereth alwayth crimeth in newthpaperth,' said Violet Elizabeth, with that air of superior knowledge which the Outlaws always found so maddening in one of her extreme youth. 'Thereth crimeth and polithe an' people goin' to prithon. If you're goin' to have a real newthpaper, thomebody ought to do a crime.'

'All right,' said William, nettled by this terrible child's invasion of his editorial province. 'All right. Go an' do one then!'

William in Trouble by Richmal Crompton

BEDTIME

Five minutes, five minutes more, please!
    Let me stay five minutes more!
Can't I just finish the castle
    I'm building here on the floor?
Can't I just finish the story
    I'm reading here in my book?
Can't I just finish this bead-chain –
    It *almost* is finished, look!
Can't I just finish this game, please?
    When a game's once begun
It's a pity never to find out
    Whether you've lost or won.
Can't I just stay five minutes?
    Well, can't I stay just four?
Three minutes, then? two minutes?
    Can't I stay *one* minute more?

                        Eleanor Farjeon

PLAYGROUNDS

In summer I am very glad
   We children are so small,
For we can see a thousand things
   That men can't see at all.

They don't know much about the moss
   And all the stones they pass:
They never lie and play among
   The forests in the grass:

They walk about a long way off:
   And, when we're at the sea,
Let father stoop as best he can
   He can't find things like me.

But, when the snow is on the ground
   And all the puddles freeze,
I wish that I were very tall,
   High up above the trees.

               Sir Lawrence Alma-Tadema

DEEP DEPRESSIONS

Mummie went out shopping,
An' Mummie bought for me
A simply lovely sunshade
As grown-up as can be.
When I went out on Sunday
I thought it would be fun
To take my sunshade with me BUT
There wasn't any sun!

On Monday and on Tuesday
It simply poured with rain,
On Wednesday and Thursday
It poured and poured again.
Friday was a dry day
But very dull and grey,
The sky was raining CATS and DOGS
The whole of Saturday.

'Twas awfully sweet of Mummie
But I think I'd better tell her
Next time she goes out shopping
To change it for a 'brella!

Jennie Dunbar

'I don't know anything about boys,' she said slowly. 'Could you keep a secret, if I told you one? It's a great secret, I don't know what I should do if anyone found it out. I believe I should die!' She said the last sentence quite fiercely.

Dickon looked more puzzled than ever and even rubbed his hand over his rough head again, but he answered good-humouredly.

'I'm keepin' secrets all th' time,' he said. 'If I couldn't keep secrets from th' other lads, secrets about foxes' cubs, an' birds' nests, an' wild things' holes, there'd be naught safe on th' moor. Aye, I can keep secrets.'

Mistress Mary did not mean to put out her hand and clutch his sleeve, but she did it.

'I've stolen a garden,' she said very fast. 'It isn't mine. It isn't anybody's. Nobody wants it, nobody cares for it, nobody ever goes into it. Perhaps everything is dead in it already; I don't know.'

The Secret Garden by Frances Hodgson Burnett

BEFORE TEA

Emmeline
Has not been seen
For more than a week. She slipped between
The two tall trees at the end of the green . . .
We all went after her. *'Emmeline!'*

'Emmeline,
I didn't mean –
I only said that your hands weren't clean.'
We went to the trees at the end of the green . . .
But Emmeline
Was not to be seen.

Emmeline
Came slipping between
The two tall trees at the end of the green.
We all ran up to her. 'Emmeline!
Where have you been?
Where have you been?
Why, it's more than a week!' And Emmeline
Said, 'Sillies, I went and saw the Queen.
She says my hands are *purfickly* clean!'

A. A. Milne

BOXING DAY

I only had an orange and just a tiny fig,
And then perhaps an apple – it wasn't very big.
I *think* I had some almonds – and raisins, too,
    as well –
But just how many grapes I had is more than I
    can tell.
And hardly any choc'lates – well, only three or
    four –
And nine or ten brazil nuts – I know it wasn't
    more.
It's queer I feel so giddy and wuzzy in the
head.
I'll really be quite thankful when they say it's
    time for bed!

       *   *   *

(No, thank you, I don't want any supper!)

                                    Jennie Dunbar

Curly locks, Curly locks,
  Wilt thou be mine?
Thou shalt not wash dishes
  Nor yet feed the swine,
But sit on a cushion
  And sew a fine seam,
And feed upon strawberries,
  Sugar and cream.

Christina herself had troubled recollections of her childhood. Looked after by nannies and private tutors, taking her meals with servants, travelling with bodyguards, she had few friends of her own age. She became an uncommunicative child whose awkwardness and natural shyness were often misunderstood as rudeness and put people off. When she was five years old, she suddenly stopped speaking to anyone at all. Tina consulted child psychologists in Zurich, who diagnosed mercurial mutism – an attention-seeking silence often associated with insecure and overprotected children. Years later, confronting this episode, Christina said, 'I guess I didn't talk because I didn't have anything to say.' ('If she had just said "hello" we could have saved $20,000,' Tina complained when she heard the explanation.) 'I keep reading that my dolls were dressed by Dior in the latest fashions from Paris,' Christina would later tell her first husband, Joseph Bolker. 'And they were very nice, but expensive dolls can't replace absent parents when you're four years old.'

Heiress: The Story of Christina Onassis
by Nigel Dempster

There were good times, too. A lot of picnics, especially around Labor Day: big containers of lemonade, homemade pies and fried chicken, and a whole hog spitted up on the barbecue, crackling and turning. Sometimes Mr Bootsy Whitelaw would play, and maybe there'd be another man playing a drum with him, or someone with a trumpet. It was just country music, picnic music – not the blues or anything. Mr Bootsy had big feet, big

lips, big flaring nostrils and big, big bubble eyes that just popped out of his head when he played the trombone. Everybody sort of laughed about how he looked – like a frog, I guess. But he could blow. And if I was there, I would always sing along and dance around to his music: I would entertain. I was just a little girl, little Anna Mae, and I'd shout, 'Come on, everybody, sing with Mr Bootsy!' That was the first 'live band' I ever saw, and I liked it.

I, Tina by Tina Turner and Kurt Loder

'My whole upbringing [forced me] to mask my feelings,' Marlene Dietrich wrote later.

'The last slap I had from my mother was because of that. I was having dancing lessons and had to dance with everyone in the room, including a young man I did not like. I made a long face. Mother saw it and slapped me as soon as we were alone. "You must not show your feelings, it is bad manners," she said.'

Dietrich by Donald Spoto

Graceful trees and bushes were growing along the riverbanks – weeping willows and alders and tall clumps of rhododendrons with their pink and red and mauve blossoms. In the meadows there were thousands of buttercups.

'*There!*' cried Mr Wonka, dancing up and down and pointing his gold-topped cane at the great brown river. 'It's *all* chocolate! Every drop of that river is hot melted chocolate of the finest quality. The *very* finest quality. There's enough chocolate in there to fill *every* bathtub in the *entire* country! *And* all the swimming pools as well! Isn't it *terrific*? And just look at my pipes! They suck up the chocolate and carry it away to all the other rooms in the factory where it is needed! Thousands of gallons an hour, my dear children! Thousands and thousands of gallons!'

Charlie and the Chocolate Factory by Roald Dahl

'Bathing by moonlight! Walking as far as one dared up the long, narrow path to the moon, the alfresco dinners with a lamp on the table and no moths or insects ever to trouble us. Herbert in grand form, Max [Beerbohm] in a sweetpea-purple and mauve smoking-suit – the fun of it. Primroses like a carpet and tamarisk for a wall, and the beat and suck of the tide, and the rooks overhead fussing, and Maud reading aloud, and sometimes Harry Cust with his wit, out-vying Maud and hers, and laughter and youth – Oh God! – and then we sang and drifted to bed. . . . The first motor too – either Maud or Herbert brought it triumphantly down from London. A Panhard, one mouse-power. The door at the back like a pony cart. Excellent car on the straight, but stopped dead and ran back at the slightest incline.'

Bemused, entranced, half asleep, Diana would linger on the fringes of this enchanted circle, praying that nobody would notice her and send her off to bed.

Diana Cooper by Philip Ziegler

A   was an apple pie;

B   bit it;

C   cut it;

D   dealt it;

E   eat (ate) it;

F   fought for it;

G   got it;

H   had it;

I   inked it;

J   joined it;

K   kept it;

L   longed for it;

M   mourned for it;

N   nodded at it;

O   opened it;

P   peeped in it;

Q   quartered it;

R   ran for it;

S   stole it;

T   took it;

V   viewed it;

W   wanted it;

X, Y, Z, and ampersand

All wished for a piece in hand.

Grace was the only Kelly child not robustly healthy; Kell recalled that she was made to drink the blood juice of the family roast 'to build her up'. Her sickly state affected her personality, made her even shyer and more withdrawn than she already was. Jack Kelly, for one, couldn't understand this un-Kelly-like behaviour, and he offered little 'Gracie' scant sympathy. He was frequently heard to ask his wife, 'What's Grace snivelling about now?'

Most of Grace's later drives in life would be motivated by a deep-seated need for her father's love and approbation, but it seemed that there was nothing she could do to impress him. Even after Grace won an Oscar, Jack Kelly told the press, 'I always thought it would be Peggy. Anything Grace could do, Peggy could do better. How do you figure these things?'

> *Grace: The Secret Lives of a Princess*
> by James Spada

POLITENESS

If people ask me,
I always tell them:
'Quite well, thank you, I'm very glad to say.'
If people ask me,
I always answer,
'Quite well, thank you, how are you to-day?'
I always answer,
I always tell them,
If they ask me
Politely . . . .
BUT SOMETIMES
     I wish
          That they wouldn't.

A. A. Milne

I didn't want to go to kindergarten because
the boys pulled up my skirt, so I began to
wear overalls. I behaved badly in class and was
put into the cloakroom during milk and
graham crackers for clowning and being
disruptive. My only real goal was to get home

69

by midmorning and be with my mother.

Since she lived on the property, my escapes were easy enough, and back in her room I comforted myself listening to Uncle Don's Nursery Rhymes, having lovely tea parties with my dollies, scribbling in my Three Little Piggies book, or helping Mother with chores. Outside I played alone, climbing oak trees, picking and eating the Miner's lettuce which grew in abundance at the base of the redwood trees, taking my Raggedy Ann for walks.

And a Voice to Sing With: A Memoir by Joan Baez

ON THE BANISTERS

Sliding down the banisters,
    The day it rained all day,
We played at flying fairies
    Coming down a rainbow ray.
I slit my frock a little bit,
    And Billy tore the mat –
But fairies aren't particular
    About such things as that.

Sliding down the banisters
  The day it rained all day,
We played at sailing aeroplanes
  To countries miles away.
I hurt my hand a little bit,
  And Billy bumped his nose,
But airmen take no notice,
  Of such little things as those.

Sliding down the banisters
  The day it rained all day,
We played at swings and switchbacks
  Like they have Olympia way.
Then folks came in, all wet and cross,
  And made us stop our play.
But oh, we did enjoy ourselves
  The day it rained all day.

Margaret E. Gibbs

As a child they called her not Agnes, but Gonxha, 'flower bud' in Albanian, for she was pink and plump. She was neat and tidy and always helpful. Lazar confessed that as a

child he had a great weakness for confectionery and desserts, and often made nocturnal visits to the kitchen cupboard. Gonxha was the only one who never stole the jam. She unfailingly reminded her brother that he should touch no food after midnight if they were to attend mass in the morning, but she never complained about these expeditions to their mother.

Mother Teresa by Navin Chawla

What are little boys made of?
What are little boys made of?
Frogs and snails
And puppy-dogs' tails,
That's what little boys are made of.

What are little girls made of?
What are little girls made of?
Sugar and spice
And all things nice,
That's what little girls are made of.

Hopes, Fears and Dreams

I want to go aboard my ship, and sail and sail
　　away –
To see the whales a-spouting and the porpoises
　　at play;
To meet Atlantic rollers with their wild and
　　mighty sweep –
I want to know the dangers and the wonders
　　of the deep.

I want to see tall icebergs, all a-sparkle,
　　drifting by
With surf about their buttresses, their spires
　　against the sky,
To make my voyage northwards till we're fast
　　amid the floe
Where the white bear prowls around us,
　　hunting seals across the snow.

I want to land on coral isles, far in the ocean
　　blue,
To battle round the dreadful Horn as all stout
　　seamen do.
But since I'm not quite old enough I sometimes
　　dream instead,
And make myself adventures though they're
　　only in my head.

　　　　　　　　　　　　　　　　　W. K. Holmes

She wished that she had a brother or sister. She wished that she was allowed to play with the children from the village on the other side of the moat. But, because she was a Princess, she could only give them a Royal wave from the distance. Eventually she went for a walk alone in the garden and ran under the trees trying to catch the copper leaves as they drifted down from the branches. She knew that if you catch a falling leaf before it touches the ground you can make a wish and the wish will come true. But every time that the Princess was sure she had a leaf in her hands a little breeze whisked it away and she was left with nothing.

The Princess and the Unicorn
by Marika Hanbury Tenison

THE REASON WHY

I can't cry,
I shan't cry,
I'm *much* too big to-day!

I do feel rarver like it though
'cos Ann won't stop and play,

An' both my new balloons have
gone and flewed theirselves away!

BUT
I don't cry,
I *won't* cry,
I mustn't cry to-day!
I've tumbled down and scraped my knees,
    and made a norful mess
Of both my clean white sandals, and
    I've spoilt my nice new dress.

I'm trying very hard to smile – a grown-up
    never cries –
But p'raps the sun is rarver strong – there's
    water in my eyes.

And don't you know I *always* laugh in this
   queer choky way?

BUT
I shan't cry,
I *can't* cry,
I'm five years old to-day!

Jennie Dunbar

Golden slumbers kiss your eyes,
Smiles awake you when you rise.
Sleep, pretty wantons, do not cry,
And I will sing you a lullaby:
Rock them, rock them, lullaby.

Care is heavy, therefore sleep you;
You are care, and care must keep you.
Sleep, pretty wantons, do not cry,
And I will sing you a lullaby:
Rock them, rock them, lullaby.

Thomas Dekker

'If you knew Time as well as I do,' said the Hatter, 'you wouldn't talk about wasting *it*. It's *him*.'

'I don't know what you mean,' said Alice.

'Of course you don't!' the Hatter said, tossing his head contemptuously. 'I daresay you never spoke to Time!'

'Perhaps not,' Alice cautiously replied: 'but I know I have to beat time when I learn music.'

'Ah! that accounts for it,' said the Hatter. 'He won't stand beating. Now, if you only kept on good terms with him, he'd do almost anything you liked with the clock. For instance, suppose it were nine o'clock in the morning, just time to begin lessons: you'd only have to whisper a hint to Time, and round goes the clock in a twinkling! Half-past one, time for dinner!'

('I only wish it was,' the March Hare said to itself in a whisper.)

'That would be grand, certainly,' said Alice thoughtfully: 'but then – I shouldn't be hungry for it, you know.'

Alice's Adventures in Wonderland
by Lewis Carroll

LITTLE GIRL

I will build you a house
If you do not cry,
A house, little girl,
As tall as the sky.

I will build you a house
Of golden dates,
The freshest of all
For the steps and gates.

I will furnish the house,
For you and for me
With walnuts and hazels
Fresh from the tree.

I will build you a house,
And when it is done
I will roof it with grapes
To keep out the sun.

Rose Fyleman (from an Arabian nursery rhyme)

But I loved my mother. Oh . . . I remember she used to sit in the window of the kitchen when she was making dinner on Sundays, and always stare out at the sky. And I used to just watch her. I thought she was so pretty, like a young, black squaw: very small, with a little pointed nose, thin lips, big teeth, a bit of gold in them. I saw her in her beauty there, sitting in that window. I watched her hands, her feet, the way she smoothed her hair. I knew her toe-nails, and how her toes curved. And her smell: I always went to her chair when she left it so I could smell her aroma – clean, sweet, very feminine. She was 'woman' to me – what a woman was. I knew every darned thing about her. I loved her and she didn't even realise it. I'd look at her and think 'Oh, she's really pretty. I wish . . .' And I'd wish and I'd wish. But I never got that wish. My mother wasn't mean to me, but she wasn't warm, she wasn't close, the way she was with Alline. She just didn't want me. But she was my mother, and I loved her.

I, Tina by Tina Turner and Kurt Loder

IT'S A LONG WAY UP IN THE DARK

I know there are Bears at the bend of the stairs,
I'll whistle to show them that nobody cares.
I'll walk past them slowly then p'raps it'll
    show
Those Bears I'm not frightened (in case they
    don't know).

That bend *was* exciting, not one single Bear
(Because I was whistling) came out of its lair.

I'm safe in my bedroom, I've shut the door
    tight,
And finished undressing and turned out the
    light.

And as for those Bears at the bend of the stairs
They can't touch me now 'cos I've
    said
        all
            my
                prayers!

Jennie Dunbar

81

Night-times were worst. As children, Diana and her brother Charles were afraid of the dark and they insisted that the landing light was left on or a candle lit in their rooms. With the wind whistling in the trees outside their window and the night-time cries of owls and other creatures, Park House could be a creepy place for a child. One evening when their father casually mentioned that a murderer was on the loose in the vicinity, the children were too terrified to sleep, listening anxiously to every rattle, creak and squeak in the silent house. Diana daubed luminous paint on the eyes of her cuddly green hippo so that at night it seemed as though he was keeping watch and looking after her.

Diana: Her True Story by Andrew Morton

Wendy was almost speechless with delight at the thought of sitting beside a boy who knew fairies, and after a minute said, 'Peter, do you really know fairies?'

'Yes, but they're nearly all dead now. You see, Wendy, when the first baby laughed for the first time, its laugh broke into a thousand pieces, and they all went skipping about, and that was the beginning of fairies. And now, whenever a new baby is born, its first laugh becomes a fairy. So there ought to be a fairy for every little boy and girl, but there isn't. You see, children know such a lot now. They soon won't believe in fairies, and whenever a child says, "I don't believe in fairies", there's a fairy somewhere that falls down dead.'. . .

'But, Peter,' continued Wendy, 'if you don't live with the fairies, where do you live?

'I live with the Lost Boys.'

'Who are they?'

'Why, they are the children who fall out of their perambulators when their nurses are looking the other way. If they are not claimed within seven days, they are sent far away to the Never-Never-Never-Land to defray expenses. I'm their Captain.'

Peter Pan by J. M. Barrie

After lunch, we would have Rest, all lying on the bare floorboards in neat rows like sardines while we were read a story. Those with colds 'hung', lying on tummies on desks and tables with heads hanging over the edge, and great nose-blowings when Rest was over. I longed for a cold, but never had one. I also longed for a plate, a brace to go round my teeth, which could be clacked in and out and gave one an air of superior intelligence – but my teeth were straight, and I had to make do with bent kirbigrips twisted round my back teeth. Crazes came and went – skipping games, conkers, diabolos and jacks, and collecting inn-signs.

Stare Back and Smile by Joanna Lumley

I daydreamed chiefly about beauty. I dreamed of myself becoming so beautiful that people would turn to look at me when I passed. And I dreamed of colours – scarlet, gold, green, white. I dreamed of myself walking proudly in beautiful clothes and being admired by everyone and overhearing words of praise. I made up the praises and repeated them aloud as if someone else were saying them.

Daydreaming made my work easier. When I was waiting on the table in one of the poverty-stricken, unhappy homes where I lived, I would daydream I was a waitress in an elegant hotel, dressed in a white waitress uniform, and everybody who entered the grand dining room where I was serving would stop to look at me and openly admire me.

I never daydreamed about love, even after I fell in love the first time. This was when I was around eight. I fell in love with a boy named George who was a year older. We used to hide in the grass together until he got frightened and jumped up and ran away.

My Story by Marilyn Monroe

'I can't help crowing when I'm pleased with myself. One girl is more use than twenty boys.'

This was rather clever of Peter, and at these sensible words Wendy got up again. She even offered to give Peter a kiss if he liked. Peter looked puzzled, but seeing the thimble on Wendy's finger, he thought she meant to give him that, and held out his hand for it. Now Wendy saw at a glance that the poor boy did not even know what a kiss was, but being a nice little girl, of motherly disposition, she did not hurt his feelings by laughing at him, but simply placed the thimble on his finger.

Peter admired the thimble very much. 'Shall I give you a kiss?' he asked, and jerking a button off his coat, solemnly presented it to her.

Wendy at once fastened it on a chain which she wore round her neck, and, forgetting the puzzle in his mind, she once more asked him for a kiss.

Immediately he returned the thimble. 'Oh! I didn't mean a kiss, I meant a thimble!'

'What's that?' he asked.

'It's like this,' replied Wendy, and gently

kissed his cheek.

'Oh!' cried Peter, 'how nice!' and he began to give her thimbles in return, and ever afterwards he called a kiss a thimble, and a thimble a kiss.

Peter Pan by J. M. Barrie

I'D LOVE TO BE A FAIRY'S CHILD

Children born of fairy stock
Never need for shirt or frock,
Never want for food or fire,
Always get their heart's desire:
Jingle pockets full of gold,
Marry when they're seven years old,
Every fairy child may keep
Two strong ponies and ten sheep:
All have houses, each his own,
Built of brick or granite stone;
They live on cherries, they run wild –
I'd love to be a fairy's child.

Robert Graves

TO MY MOTHER

You too, my mother, read my rhymes
For love of unforgotten times,
And you may chance to hear once more
The little feet along the floor.

Robert Louis Stevenson

Many fairies are said to be masters of magic. Their presents, which at first look like rubbish, may turn into jewels or gold; or presents of jewels and gold may turn into rubbish. Some of them are able to appear and disappear at will, though people can penetrate their disguise by applying a magic eye ointment made by the fairies themselves, or by holding a four-leafed clover. Some can fly, though few have wings. Usually they ride on ragwort stalks, or levitate themselves by wearing magic caps or by reciting spells.

Folklore, Myths and Legends of Britain

One of the poor child's many duties was to go twice a day and draw water from a spring a good half-mile away, bringing it back in a large pitcher. One day when she was at the spring an old woman came up and begged for a drink.

'Why, certainly, good mother,' the pretty lass replied. Rinsing her pitcher, she drew some water from the cleanest part of the spring and handed it to the dame, lifting up the jug so that she might drink the more easily.

Now this old woman was a fairy, who had taken the form of a poor village dame to see just how far the girl's good nature would go. 'You are so pretty,' she said, when she had finished drinking, 'and so polite, that I am determined to bestow a gift upon you. This is the boon I grant you: with every word that you utter there shall fall from your mouth either a flower or a precious stone.'

When the girl reached home she was scolded by her mother for being so long in coming back from the spring.

'I am sorry to have been so long, mother,' said the poor child.

As she spoke these words there fell from her mouth three roses, three pearls and three diamonds.

'What's this?' cried her mother; 'did I see pearls and diamonds dropping out of your mouth? What does this mean, dear daughter?' (This was the first time she had ever addressed her daughter affectionately.)

Perrault's Fairy Tales

Suddenly a clear rippling little sound broke out near her and she turned round. She was standing a few feet from a young apple-tree, and the robin had flown on to one of its branches and had burst out into a scrap of a song. Ben Weatherstaff laughed outright.

'What did he do that for?' asked Mary.

'He's made up his mind to make friends with thee,' replied Ben. 'Dang me if he hasn't took a fancy to thee.'

'To me?' said Mary, and she moved towards the little tree softly and looked up.

'Would you make friends with me?' she said to the robin, just as if she were speaking to a person. 'Would you?' And she did not say it either in her hard little voice or in her imperious Indian voice, but in a tone so soft and eager and coaxing that Ben Weatherstaff was as surprised as she had been when she heard him whistle.

'Why,' he cried out, 'tha' said that as nice an' human as if tha' was a real child instead of a sharp old woman. Tha' said it almost like Dickon talks to his wild things on th' moor.'

The Secret Garden by Frances Hodgson Burnett

Of course it was not always like this. Mother and child quarrelled from the beginning, each possessing parallel but divergent wills. Like sister-ships they were hauled together in the same emotional estuary while riding strong and contrary currents. I suppose this to be the fate of nearly all parents: mothers and daughters share the same prison cells, meshed in rival jealousies and irritations;

while fathers, hoping to be their daughters' liberators, double-lock them with silken keys.

But I like to remember the two in the lamplit evenings by the cottage fire, during the first of those newborn weeks, the child feeding at the breast, the sleepy adjusting fingers, the bunting mouth, the little grunts of concentration and bliss. I don't think I've ever seen them since in such a state of single-minded agreement, so quietly immersed in their shared purposes.

Two Women by Laurie Lee

My dear daughter, be very good. Do not bump yourself. Do not eat matches. Do not play with scissors or cats. Do not forget your dad. Sleep when your mother wishes it. Love us both. Try to know how we love you. That you will never learn. Goodnight and God keep you, and bless you.

Your Dad

Letter by Richard Harding Davis

SOURCES AND ACKNOWLEDGEMENTS

Extracts and poems reproduced by
permission are listed below.

Baez, Joan, *And a Voice to Sing With* (copyright ©
1987 by Joan Baez; reprinted by permission of
Simon & Schuster Inc.)

Chawla, Navin, *Mother Teresa* (by permission of
Sinclair-Stevenson and Aitken, Stone & Wylie Ltd)

Crompton, Richmal, *William in Trouble* (Pan
Macmillan Children's Books)

Dahl, Roald, *Charlie and the Chocolate Factory* (by
permission of Murray Pollinger and Penguin
Books Ltd)

de la Mare, Walter, 'The Birthnight' (The Literary
Trustees of Walter de la Mare and The Society of
Authors as their representative)

Dempster, Nigel, *Heiress: The Story of Christina
Onassis* (Weidenfeld & Nicolson)

Drabble, Margaret, *The Millstone* (Weidenfeld &
Nicolson)

Edwards, Anne, *Shirley Temple: American Princess* (by
permission of Rogers, Coleridge & White Ltd)

Edwards, Dorothy, *My Naughty Little Sister*

Less Deceived, by permission of The Marvell Press, England)

Leaming, Barbara, *Bette Davis* (Weidenfeld & Nicolson)

Lee, Laurie, *Two Women* (Penguin Books 1984; first published by André Deutsch; copyright © Laurie Lee 1983; reproduced by permission of Penguin Books Ltd)

Lumley, Joanna, *Stare Back and Smile* (published by Michael Joseph; reprinted by permission of David Higham Associates)

Milne, A. A., 'Before Tea', 'Politeness' and 'Halfway Down the Stairs' from *When We Were Very Young* (reprinted by permission of Methuen Children's Books)

Monroe, Marilyn, *My Story* (Stein & Day, NY)

Morton, Andrew, *Diana: Her True Story* (Michael O'Mara Books Ltd)

Opie, Iona and Tatem, Moira, *Dictionary of Superstitions* (copyright © Iona Opie and Moira Tatem 1989; by permission of Oxford University Press)

Raeburn, Anna, *Talking to Myself* (Hamish Hamilton, 1984; copyright © Anna Raeburn 1984; reproduced by permission of Hamish Hamilton Ltd)

Redgrave, Vanessa, *An Autobiography* (Hutchinson)

Sands, Frederick and Broman, Sven, *The Divine Garbo* (Sidgwick & Jackson)

Spada, James, *Grace* (Sidgwick & Jackson)

Spender, Stephen, 'To My Daughter' (from *Collected Poems 1928–1985* by Stephen Spender, published by Faber & Faber Ltd)

Spoto, Donald, *Dietrich* (by permission of Elaine Markson Literary Agency)

Turner, Tina, *I, Tina* (reprinted by permission of Sterling Lord Literistic, Inc.; copyright © 1986 by Tina Turner)

Walker, Alexander, *Elizabeth* (Weidenfeld & Nicolson)

Woodward, Ian, *Audrey Hepburn* (Virgin/Henry Holt)

Ziegler, Philip, *Diana Cooper* (Hamish Hamilton, 1987; copyright © Philip Ziegler, 1987; reproduced by permission of Hamish Hamilton Ltd)